Today's America

Today's America

Things America
doesn't like to talk about

David Garza

To order additional copies of this book, contact:
Xlibris
1-888-795-4274
www.Xlibris.com
Orders@Xlibris.com
807240

CONTENTS

CHAPTER 1

The Current State of Americans

I am old enough to remember what it's like to see America come out of the tail end of a white racist America in the late sixties and early seventies. America did make some huge progress as a society from the eighties to the two thousands and I'm young enough to be concerned about the future of this new black racially dominated America.

It's a place in which all a black person has to do is make an accusation of discrimination of any kind whatsoever, and society bows down and caters to them.

You see, I can honestly make this statement without anybody judging me. I am not black, and I am not white.

I am of Mexican-American heritage. If you speak Spanish, "Soy un Tejano de sangre puro!" that means that I am a Tex-Mex.

Why should we Americans who are not fixated on racism or skin color be forced to watch America change from a then-white racist society to a now-black racist society? Perhaps the black-and white-skin-colored people in America have forgotten that there are also brown-, yellow-, and red-skin-colored people here in the United States.

I do not have white friends, and I do not have black friends. I do not have brown, yellow, or red friends either. I just have friends. Some of them happen to be white, some of them are black, some of them are brown, and some of them are yellow.

I do not pick my friends by the color of their skin. I judge my friends by the actions of their good deeds and their contributions to society.

It doesn't matter if you are white, black, brown, yellow, or red. If you have to introduce your friends as "This is my white [black, Mexican, or Asian] friend," you are more than likely a racist; and you should look for some new friends.

When I introduce a new friend to my old friends, the old friends don't care about the skin color of the new friend.

That is the type of people that you should be surrounding yourself with.

In my lifetime, I have seen this country go from a society in which white people could make comments either openly or under their breath and get away with it. Now, we're in a society in which the roles have been reversed, and black people are the ones who can now make statements under their breath or openly and get away with it.

The really sad part is that you have these people who hide under the guise of "black activism." In reality, what they really want is to have what the white man used to have: total control.

In a society such as America, everybody is *equal* irregardless of your skin color, gender, or sexual preference.

The black activist do not see it this way.

Do you need proof?

Every black person in the United States knows what BET (Black Entertainment Television), the NAACP (National Association for the Advancement of Colored

People), and black Twitter are. I ask you, where are WET (White Entertainment Television), NAAWP (National Association for Advancement of White People), or white Twitter? They do not exist because if they did they would be deemed as white supremacist, white nationalist, or racist organizations.

Equal means equal!

Want more proof?

I dare you to say the word *nigger* in public. I do it once a week just to keep everybody on their toes. You should see the look of horror on white people's faces when I say it. They have been browbeaten into submission. They have become the more docile race because they have let black Americans stifle their free speech.

Let me say that again.

Caucasians no longer have freedom of speech. At the same time, a black person can call a white person a honky, cracker, or Whitey; and everything is OK.

In the early seventies, I was called a wetback so many times that I actually thought I was a wetback (especially when all four of my grandparents spoke Spanish as a first language). I am a fourth-generation American in both my mother's and father's bloodlines.

The United States Constitution says, "All men are created equal." Nowhere does it say that all men are created equal, but we're going to give the black people a little more because they were once oppressed.

No favoritisms should be granted to black, white, feminists, or gay people.

Equal means just that—equal.

As an American, I am *happy* to see that feminists, black, and gay Americans have made progress in their social standings. I am now anxiously waiting for them to start acting like grown-ups and quit acting like little children claiming that they don't have a spot at the big kids' table. You've done it. You're at the big kids' table now. For the sake of the rest of America, please start acting accordingly.

CHAPTER 2

My Experiences in Different Regions of America

I've been lucky enough to be able to travel to different regions of the United States throughout my life. In my early teens, I spent three summers on a dairy farm outside of Lafayette, Louisiana, in a then-small town named Youngsville.

In my early twenties, I traveled up and down the East Coast and New England regions of America working as a concert venue roadie for Paul McCartney. I was offered an opportunity to accompany McCartney across the Atlantic Ocean back to the United Kingdom. For personal reasons, I chose to stay in the United States; and I picked up odd jobs across the United States while working my way back toward my hometown of Houston, Texas.

As such, I have been able to make some pretty astute observations:

1) No region of the country is perfect. Every region has its faults.

2) There are some "pockets" in the northeastern region of the country that still seem to have some tensions in regard to racism. By and large, I don't think racism is as prevalent as some of these black activists make the situation out to be. In regard to the West Coast racism, I think a lot of that is based on the financial inequality that exists there as well as the clash of the political ideologies of progressive and liberals trying to overtake conservative values. If you put all those opposing forces in the same region of the country, of course, you're going to have some bickering back-and-forth disagreements, jealousy, and envy. It would be irresponsible for anybody to come up with a different conclusion other than the one that I just described.

3) I grew up in the Gulf Coast region of the country. One of the things I realized as I became a teenager was that almost all the states that border the Gulf of Mexico raise their children with the same moral standards as the neighboring states. Of course, you're

going to have some differences here and there; but by and large, all Gulf state people tend to think alike. Their train of thought is "I just want to go to work and make money to raise my family. I'm not worried about you and your private business, so please don't be worried about me and my private business."

We say this with kindness and not out of arrogance, spite, or malice. We have the capability of saying, "That's none of my business" and then just walk away because we know that it truly is none of our concern and also that we are going to see that person at the next community picnic, barbecue, fish fry, crawfish boil, quinceañera, etc. For those of you who do not know what a quinceañera is, it is a celebration of a girl's fifteenth birthday. It marks the transition from a child into a young woman. It is a formal event, and it usually starts off with a mass or service at the local church and then moves into a reception hall. It is like a sweet sixteen, except we do it at the age of fifteen. It is a huge event not only for the young lady but also for the community as a whole, so much so that many Anglo American teenage girls who live in South and West Texas will many times forego a sweet sixteen in lieu of a quinceañera. A typical quinceañera can have anywhere from two hundred to five hundred guests. The guests are treated to live music, food, alcohol, and dancing. The lineage of the quinceañera can be traced all the way back to the Aztec culture in 500 BC.

People in the Gulf Coast region know how to live and let live. They have the understanding that "we do not always have to agree, but we do have to be neighbors." This seems to be a trait and an inherent quality instilled into all the Gulf Coast residents.

There seems to be a very different trait in the people of the New England, Chicago, and California regions of the country. They are forever trying to push their train of thought and ideologies to the person next to them. If you have a different train of thought or idea than them, they immediately start to accost, bully, browbeat, berate, intimidate, publicly shame, and sometimes physically assault you.

That is something you just do not experience in Florida, Alabama, Mississippi, Louisiana, and Texas. Even in the neighboring states of Georgia, Arkansas, Oklahoma, and New Mexico, everybody gets along fairly well. Like I mentioned earlier, you are always going to have those isolated cases of disagreement.

Take Texas, for example. I know from personal experience, because I grew up in Texas, that black-, white-, brown-, yellow-, and red-skinned people all live together in perfect harmony; and it should come as no surprise. The name Texas was taken from the Spanish word Tejas. The Spanish settlers in the 1500s took the word from a local Native American tribe's vocabulary. *Tejas* means *allies* or *friendly people*. That's right—the word Texas means *friendly people*. Look it up!

CHAPTER 3

Basic Texas History

For those of you who fell asleep during the Texas-history portion of your education or perhaps you were raised in a school district that chose not to teach Texas's history, there have been six nations that have laid claim to the land of Texas:

- Spain: 1519–1685, 1690–1821

- France: 1685–1690

- Mexico: 1821–1836

- Republic of Texas: 1836–1845

- United States: 1845–1861, 1865–present

- Confederate States of America: 1861-1865

Spain and the United States flags are the only two flags to fly in two separate regimes during the history of Texas.

Since the early 1500s, there have been six different nations' flags flown over the land of Texas. That is where the Theme/Amusement Park Six Flags got its name. It was founded in Arlington, Texas, on August 5, 1961. The original name was Six Flags over Texas.

In the 1800s, the Texas region was a lot larger than it is today. General/Presidente' Antonio Lopez de Santa Anna defeated the Texians at the Battle of the Alamo. The Battle took place from February 23, 1836-March 6, 1836. A few of the famous people that perished in the battle are Lieutenant Colonel William Barret "Buck" Travis, Colonel James "Jim" Bowie and Colonel David "Davy" Crockett. You may have seen or heard of a Bowie knife. The knife was named after Jim Bowie. Upon losing his seat in the House of Representative from the State of Tennessee, Davy Crockett penned one of the more famous quotes in U.S. and Texas history, "Since you have chosen to elect a man with a timber toe to succeed me, you may all go to hell and I will go to Texas."

On April 21, 1836, General Sam Houston with 800 members of the Texian Army defeated General/Presidente Santa Anna's Mexican Army of approximately 1,500 men at the battlegrounds of San Jacinto approximately twenty-two miles from present-day downtown Houston. The Texians could be heard shouting the battle cry, "Remember the Alamo!"

Texas declared itself an independent republic and immediately elected Sam Houston as the first president of the Republic of Texas. The Texas Constitution mandates that a presidential term shall last only three years and that no president shall serve consecutive terms in office. Upon completing his first term as president (1836–1838), Sam Houston left the office; and Mirabeau B. Lamar was elected as Texas's second president (1838–1841). Lamar had served as an officer with the rank of Colonel in the Texian Army under Houston during the Texas Independence Revolution.

Houston campaigned and was elected president for a second term (1841–1844), serving as the third president of Texas. During his second term, Houston saw the writing on the wall and laid the foundation for Texas to join the United States. The fourth and final president of Texas, Anson Jones (1844–1846), ratified the ceding of Texas to the United States on December 29, 1845. Upon Texas's joining of the United States as the twenty-eighth state, Sam Houston was once again called upon to serve Texas as one of the first two senators to represent Texas in the United States Senate (February 21, 1846–March 3, 1859). Houston's last and final service to the great land of Texas was as governor. He served as the seventh governor of Texas from December 21, 1859, to March 16, 1861.

On February 1, 1861, Texas seceded from the United States; and on March 2, 1861, two weeks before Houston's final day in office, the state of Texas joined the Confederate States of America. Houston was removed from the office of governor because he would not swear allegiance to the Confederate States.

It should come as no surprise that Sam Houston ascended to the ranks of general, president, senator, and governor or that he defeated General/Presidente Santa Anna, the Napoleon of the West. As a young man, Houston served as a first lieutenant in the United States Army under then-general Andrew Jackson. You might remember him as the president on the $20 bill.

After leaving the United States Army, they remained lifelong friends. They were such good friends that Houston named one of his sons Andrew Jackson Houston. President Andrew Jackson's quote is on President Sam Houston's headstone. The epitaph reads, "The world will take care of Houston's fame."

Going back to the date of December 29, 1845, when Texas ceded to the United States, you must remember that at that time the United States did not go west of Louisiana or Oklahoma. There were a couple of major issues involved with Texas ceding to the United States:

1) Texas was *extremely* big. In 1845, the Texas Territory was almost the same size as the United States, thereby almost doubling the landmass of the United States overnight.

2) There were no set boundaries or maps made to document the perceived boundaries. This would later lead to land conflicts with Mexico, thus ensuing to the Mexican–American War (April 25, 1846–February 2, 1848).

Wanting to bring an end to the war, then-presiding president James Polk of the United States authorized Nicholas P. Trist as chief negotiator for the United States. The *presidente* of the Mexican Republic Santa Anna authorized the following three representatives as negotiators—Don Luis Gonzaga Cuevas, Don Bernardo Couto, and Don Miguel Atristain—and on February 2,

1848, the Treaty of Guadalupe Hidalgo was signed. On March 10, 1848, the U.S. Senate ratified the "Treaty of Guadalupe Hidalgo" by a vote of thirty-eight to fourteen.

The treaty ended the Mexican–American War. The terms were as follows: Mexico gave up all claims to the Texas Territory and neighboring lands. The treaty recognized the Rio Grande as Texas's southern boundary; and in return, the United States paid Mexico $15 million. All the Mexican citizens affected by the new boundary had one year to relocate south of the new boundary to remain a Mexican citizen. They could also stay in place and become United States citizens with full voting rights. Of the affected population, 80 percent chose American citizenship. My great-grandparents were among this group of 80 percent.

You might be asking yourself, just how big of a piece of land are we talking about? The land in question included *all* or *parts* of present-day Texas, New Mexico, Arizona, California, Colorado, Nevada, Utah, Kansas, Oklahoma, and Wyoming. All this land could now become part of the United States because then-general Sam Houston had defeated General/Presidente Santa Anna.

Sam Houston lived from March 2, 1793, to July 26, 1863. During his lifetime, he defeated the Mexican Army, doubled the land size of America, became a great statesman, and served as both a federal and state elected official. He was the only American to serve as governor in two states (Texas and Tennessee) and was the only foreign head of state to serve as senator in the United States Congress. He refused to join the Confederate States of America.

The city of Houston, Texas, is named after General, President, Senator, Governor Sam Houston.

When you think about it in these terms, you have to ask yourself, why isn't Sam Houston listed as a founding father of America and why is this man not on some form of US currency? Every night when I go to sleep, I scratch my head and ponder those two questions. In my opinion, this is one of the gravest travesties in American history. How can a man who contributed so much to the formation of this half of the United States not be better acknowledged? Most people in America today don't even know who he was. That is an insult to his legacy. Everybody in the United States west of Louisiana and Oklahoma is an American citizen today because of this man's accomplishments.

Prior to the 1500s, a myriad of Native American tribes all shared the land of Texas simultaneously. Just to name some: Apache, Comanche, Cherokee, Shawnee, Kickapoo, Caddo, Tonkawa, Wichita, Lipan Apache, Alabama-Coushatta,

Atakapa, Hasinai, Kickapoo Traditional Tribe of Texas, Nadaco, Nabiti, Puebloan, Tigua, Eyeish, Nacogdoche, Akokisa, Nasoni, and Kadohadacho. There are far too many to list all of them. Keep in mind that as Anglo Americans invaded the East Coast of America, all the Native American tribes of the Eastern Coast were pushed westward until they reached the Texas Territory.

All these people lived harmoniously in the region of Texas prior to any white man stepping foot in the Americas.

With this many nomadic tribes inhabiting the land, no one tribe laid claim to the land of Texas. Everybody shared the land. Texas was declared a neutral zone by Native Americans.

It's a no brainer as to why the Spanish settlers took the Caddo Native American tribe's word of Tejas.

Texas has been a melting pot of cultures since before the 1500s. When you look at the historical timeline, it's no wonder that the Texas region and surrounding states all have a better handle on getting along with your neighbors who are of a different culture. It is in our DNA. We have over a five-hundred-year head start on the rest of the country.

Just because Texans are nice and friendly, do not get it twisted! Do not mistake our kindness for weakness. We are a land of laws. We enforce our laws. We do have the death penalty for people who commit heinous crimes. In order to receive the death penalty, you must be convicted of murdering somebody while committing a felony, e.g., armed robbery, grand larceny, rape, etc. We regularly execute both men and women who break our laws. Right now, the most important laws being broken and manipulated in Texas are the immigration laws.

Political Correctness Run Amok versus Real Racism

America has become too damn sensitive. This is the generation of coddled crybabies who were medicated on drugs like Ritalin their entire adolescent and teenage lives because their parents were told that their insurance would cover the behavioral issues with medication. Now they are off their parents' medical insurance, and they have no more prescription drugs to numb their minds. They must face the harsh reality that life isn't fair and they must do it soberly. Children who were given trophies for coming in last place are now adults. They have never had any adversity in their lives. They were never taught how to lose or how to be a gracious loser as a child. Therefore, they do not know how to handle adversity as an adult; and as such, they angrily lash out at the world for their shortcomings in life. Instead of taking responsibility for their actions, they deflect the situation and look for any reason to call somebody a racist, homophobe, xenophobic, misogynist, or misandrist. That way, they can take their negative situation that they created for themselves and somehow turn it into a positive victimhood story.

Ask yourself these questions: (1) When was the last time you heard of a man getting lynched? (2) When was the last time you heard of a man being beaten because of his skin color? (3) When was the last time you heard of a woman being raped because of her skin color? (4) When was the last time you heard of a family having their house burned because of the color of their skin? (5) When was the last time you heard of a church being burned down because of the skin color of its parishioners? I have just given you five very good instances of true racism. Pay close attention to how all five of those are tangible violent acts. They are not subjective! Notice how somebody's feelings getting hurt and "bad words" do not fit into any one of those five questions.

In my lifetime, ten presidents have sat behind the desk in the Oval Office. They are Lyndon Baines Johnson, Richard Milhous Nixon, Gerald Rudolph Ford Jr., James Earl Carter Jr., Ronald Wilson Reagan, George Herbert

Walker Bush, William Jefferson Clinton, George Walker Bush, Barack Hussein Obama II, and Donald John Trump.

I have witnessed firsthand America going through the racially divided civil rights movement in the sixties and seventies. I have lived through this once before, so I know what I am talking about. I have seen it with my eyes and heard it with my ears, so I feel extremely confident in making this next observation. Real racism is almost nonexistent in today's American society. Be careful that you don't confuse political correctness running amok and true racism. They are two entirely different things. No matter how much you may despise somebody and what they are saying, that person has the same freedom of speech that you have. That means you must listen to whatever comes out of their mouth and afford them the opportunity to speak their piece. It doesn't matter whether or not you agree with them. What matters is that you afford them the opportunity to speak their mind. You have no right to stifle anybody's freedom of speech.

Whenever I speak and offend some unsuspecting "snowflake," I recite a saying that I came up with, "The United States Supreme Court recognizes my right to freedom of speech. It does not care about your sensitive feelings." I know it comes off as a bit brash and harsh; but many times, the truth hurts.

As I mentioned earlier, much of the racism in America is all but dead. The few isolated cases that do exist are extremely rare and hard to find. However, when one of these rare isolated cases comes to light, the black activists immediately exploit the incident for their benefit by saying that racially charged incidents are on the rise.

Nothing could be further from the truth:

> There is another class of colored people who make a business of keeping the troubles, the wrongs, and the hardships of the Negro race before the public. Having learned that they are able to make a living out of their troubles, they have grown into the settled habit of advertising their wrongs—partly because they want sympathy and partly because it pays. Some of these people do not want the Negro to lose his grievances, because they do not want to lose their jobs.
>
> I am afraid that there is a certain class of race-problem solvers who don't want the patient to get well, because as long as the

disease holds out they have not only an easy means of making a living, but also an easy medium through which to make themselves prominent before the public.

Both of these quotes are from Booker T. Washington (1856–1915), African American political leader, educator, author.

In 2019, that class of colored people is now called black activist. The two most prominent black activists in America today are Al Sharpton and Jesse Jackson.

Booker T. Washington was one of America's greatest African American political leaders, and he despised race baiters and people who claimed victimhood.

I am a Mexican American, and I know these quotes. How do these historically black universities (HBUs) not have this as part of their curriculums? Why are black Americans not being taught this? The reason nobody is teaching our young black American citizens these quotes is because here in America it pays to be a victim. Rather than roll up their sleeves and put in the hard work, they find it much easier to sit down and cry, "I am a victim. Please give me something."

The scary thing is that any minority can cut and paste their self-perceived affliction into this quote and recycle it as their own, e.g., women, gays, feminists, handicapped, and so forth.

In the 2010s, black activists started to racially divide this country again just like in the 1970s. The difference this time is that there are delusional white people siding with the black activists, claiming that America is a racist society. They even coined a new phrase: *white privilege.*

White privilege and male privilege are illusions. They do not exist. If you are angry at the world because a white person or a male has had success in his life, quit being bitter. Maybe, just maybe, this person has achieved success through hard work. Have you looked into this person's background to see if their accomplishments are justly deserved? Or did you just look at this person and say, "He has something and I don't. It's because he's white [or it's because he's a male]." Here's a newsflash. America does not revolve around you. The world does not stop spinning just because you did not get your way.

In the eighties and nineties, most of the Northeastern, Midwest, and West Coast Americans were finished with black versus white racism while the Gulf Coast portion of America was dealing with the American versus Cuban immigrant ordeal and rightfully so.

Between April 15 and October 31, 1980, the then-presiding Democratic president Jimmy Carter allowed political asylum seekers from Cuba into the United States. A mass immigration of Cubans ensued. They traveled from Cuba's Mariel Harbor to the Gulf Coast states of the United States.

It was nicknamed the Mariel boatlift, and the immigrants/refugees were called Marielitos. Of the 125,000 Marielitos who migrated to Florida, an estimated 16,000 to 20,000 had criminal records and another 500 were detained for mental illness. You might remember this from the opening scene of the movie *Scarface* starring Al Pacino.

Law enforcement agents across South Florida and later the entire Gulf Coast were quick to point out that the rise in crime that swept that region of the United States was directly related to the Cuban immigration crime wave. The press dubbed the Mariel boatlift as the Cuban crime wave. The Cuban crime wave merged with gangster outlaws known as the Cocaine Cowboys. When these two groups came together, they swept across the Gulf Coast states like wildfire. Once they established their presence in the Gulf Coast states, they moved on to the rest of the United States. They set up an extensive cocaine distribution network across the United States.

Coincidentally, the bulk of the Cocaine Cowboys violence came from the Cuban crime wave. There was an endless amount of news coverage from across the United States that documented this ill-fated time in American history. When you are finished reading this article, I implore you to research the terms *Cuban crime wave* and *Cocaine Cowboys*. It is very easy to see why Cuban Americans were looked down upon as common criminals, thugs, and drug dealers at that time in US history.

On November 23, 1981 *Time Magazine* published "Paradise Lost." It is an account of the effects of both the cocaine epidemic in America and the Cuban crime wave. This is the article that woke up America. It was the first nationally published news article that shed some light on the illegal drug activities and immigration problems plaguing America on a monstrous scale in Miami and South Florida.

Keep in mind this was prior to the Internet. At that time in America, nationally publicized magazines is how Americans stayed in formed. Of all the magazines with a national publication, *Time Magazine* was considered the most prestigious magazine in America for decades.

In 1985 Florida governor Bob Graham pushed for the reimbursement of $150 million from the federal government that the state of Florida spent trying to accommodate and facilitate the needs of the Cuban immigrants.

Because of President Carter's incompetence, Ronald Reagan spent the bulk of his eight years in office cleaning up the drug issues in America. The cocaine epidemic was so bad that First Lady Nancy Reagan formed a youth organization named DARE. Their motto was "Just say no."

Years later, Fidel Castro openly bragged that he emptied his prisons and mental facilities and forced the unsuspecting United States boat owners to carry the dregs of his society along with the deserting Cubans seeking political asylum back to America.

Robert McKnight published an article in the *Miami Herald* on April 18, 2018. The title of the article was "The impact of the Mariel Boatlift Still Resonates in Florida After 38 Years." It is a reflection of past events and a glimpse as to where the city of Miami is headed today as a society because of that event. It is a good read. It is one of the many news articles out there that reflect on the Mariel boatlift and its effects on Miami Florida.

This is almost exactly what Texas and the entire southwestern border are going through today with the illegal immigration from Mexico and Central America. There is a mass immigration of people claiming political asylum from Mexico and Central America into the United States.

CHAPTER 5

The US-Mexico Border Invasion

The entire US-Mexico border measures 1,954 miles. According to the Texas Department of Transportation (TxDOT) website,

> Texas and the four bordering Mexican States of Chihuahua, Coahuila, Nuevo León and Tamaulipas share 1,254 miles of that common border and are joined by 28 international bridges and border crossings. This number includes two dams, one hand-drawn ferry, and 25 other crossings that allow commercial, vehicular and pedestrian traffic.
>
> The border crossings are vital to the economies of Texas and Mexico, and have

contributed to Mexico's status as Texas' #1 trading partner.

TxDOT recognizes the importance of the relationship between both neighbors and, since the implementation of NAFTA in 1994, is continuously seeking ways to improve the safe crossing of people and goods.

Since the state of Texas owns all public waterways in the state of Texas, the Texas Parks and Wildlife State police officers (game wardens) have jurisdiction over the Rio Grande on the US side of the river. The game wardens are forever working in concert with multiple law enforcement agencies at the US-Mexico border. Those agencies include but are not limited to the border patrol (USBP), ICE, DEA, ATF, FBI, and applicable local sheriff's offices.

In the first seven months of the 2019 fiscal year, in the Rio Grande Valley sector of Texas between Brownsville and Del Rio, US Border Patrol agents had apprehended 174,000 illegal aliens. That is more than the 162,000 illegal aliens apprehended during the entire 2018 fiscal year in that sector, and that number was up from the 2017 fiscal year. Keep in mind that this is only about 380 miles of the 1,254 miles of the Texas-Mexico border.

According to Robert Colburn, former deputy chief of the United States Border Patrol,

93 percent of these people *do not* qualify for political asylum. Fleeing your home country simply for economic reasons such as no money or lack of work does not qualify as political asylum *in any country* anywhere on the planet. This is *not* a United States' policy. This is a United Nations' policy.

There is a large percentage of people within that 93 percent with criminal records. Of these people, many of them have ties to the drug cartels and or MS-13. Because these people are nefarious miscreants, they are educated in manners of circumnavigating and manipulating the United States immigration laws. Also, very few of these illegal immigrants have had any immunizations. The bulk of the American population has been given immunizations against diseases such as the measles, smallpox, and tuberculosis. That is why you do not see cases of those diseases in the United States.

There are documented cases at the border-holding facilities that these immigrants are actually indeed carrying these diseases. Since illegal aliens have had no immunizations, from a medical standpoint, there is a strong possibility that many more of these illegal aliens are carrying these diseases in the incubation period. Because they can only be held for twenty days, many times, these illegal immigrants are released into the United States' population before any symptoms of the disease come to fruition. It only takes one or two infectious people to wreak havoc on the US population.

Any reasonable, rational human being would immediately say, "Okay, let's address this issue before it spins further out of control." For some reason, the Democratic politicians of today refuse to even admit that there is an issue at the border, let alone an invasion. Their sole mantra is "Oppose Trump on all issues at all times at all costs" while the American population suffers the consequences. As of April 2019, seven months into the fiscal year, over 500,000 illegal immigrants have been apprehended at the United States–Mexico border. Both the months of March and April have reached record highs for monthly totals. We are currently on track to reach one million apprehended illegal immigrants in the 2019 fiscal year. These are just the ones who have been caught. The United States Border Patrol estimates that one out of four or five illegal immigrants is apprehended. That means that for every one million illegal immigrants caught, approximately four to five million or more go undetected.

According to the National Center for Health Statistics, the number of babies born in the United States in 2015 was 3,978,497. The *Washington Post* reported on May 26, 2018, that the number of US-born citizens fell in 2017 to 3,853,472. That means this year more illegal aliens are entering the country than US citizens are being born.

The United States Border Patrol is not set up to accommodate that number of illegal immigrants. Many times, agents are taken off the front lines to care for the necessities of these immigrants while they are in the detention centers. Agents are spending their time on changing diapers, mixing formula, providing medical care, feeding the detainees, arranging for laundry services, and more.

The drug cartels know this. As I mentioned earlier, they are of nefarious character. They utilize this information to their benefit. The cartels will send a group of three hundred to five hundred illegal aliens at one point on the border. They know that a group this size will require all available border patrol agents in the area to be called to that location. While the border patrol officers are occupied, the cartels will move the drugs across the border approximately five or ten miles down.

It's a basic military strategy: divide and conquer. Release illegal aliens here and move the drugs over there.

On May 29, 2019, near El Paso, the United States Border Patrol apprehended 1,036 illegal aliens in one massive group as they attempted to cross the border. It is the largest single apprehension in US Border Patrol history.

In 2014, roughly 2 percent of all single males crossing the US Texas-Mexico border had a child with them. In 2019, that number had jumped up to roughly 50 percent.

Border patrol agents started to notice that some of these children were crossing the border multiple times with different guardians/parents.

Border patrol agents here in Texas have started a small pilot program. Illegal immigrants that come across the border with children are being given DNA tests to verify whether the child with them is of their bloodline.

Of the illegal immigrants who have been checked with DNA testing, roughly 30 percent of them are found to be of no blood relation. The immigrants are then asked a series of questions to explain how a child who is not blood related to them is in their custody.

The illegal immigrants are just coming clean and admitting that they were told to cross into the United States with a child and they would automatically be given citizenship. They are manipulating and scamming the system.

The Democratic politicians know this, and that is why they oppose Trump on this issue. The Democratic politician's mind-set is these people may or may not get a chance to vote but if the illegal immigrants have children here in the United States, their children will be able to vote. Since we (the Democratic Party) let them into the country, they will forever be indebted to us and freely hand us their vote for the next forty to fifty years.

It's actually a very forward way of thinking. The Democrats are looking into ways of manipulating and controlling future election outcomes.

A strong case could be made against the Democratic Party in regard to voter fraud and gerrymandering.

Chapter 6

Border Wall

If an American citizen publicly states that they want the US immigration laws upheld and enforced or that they want a *border wall*, the Democrats and social justice warriors immediately call that person a *racist*.

No, it just means that we want our laws upheld and enforced. This is the United States. You do not get to pick and choose which laws you want to obey and which laws that you do not want to obey. It doesn't work like that. If it did, everybody would stop paying their taxes; and then people would start robbing banks and committing other heinous crimes like rape and murder. These laws are here for a reason. You must obey them—all of them.

The issues with the US-Mexico border are nothing new. Upon the signing of the Treaty of Guadalupe Hidalgo,

Presidente Santa Anna was extremely unhappy with the land boundary terms and immediately wanted to challenge the new boundaries, thus, beginning a long history of disputes from both sides over the US-Mexico border. Santa Anna retired from politics in 1855, but the disputes persisted.

Since verifiable accurate records from the turn of the century are hard to come by, it is hard to pinpoint the exact time when the original border fence was built in the cities of Nogales, Arizona, and Nogales, Sonora. Different historians give different recollections as to how the fence came about. However, there are many facts that multiple historians agree upon. They are as follows:

1) This takes place during a time when international tensions were on the rise because of World War I.

2) The city of Nogales was built on the international border between Mexico and United States.

3) Half of the city was in Arizona, United States, and half of the city was in Sonora, Mexico.

4) A wire fence was erected. Some say the fence was chest high, and other say it was six feet tall.

5) In previous years, multiple pedestrians had been shot while attempting to cross the international border.

6) The fence was erected to control pedestrian foot traffic in an attempt to ease international tensions.

7) The fence ran the entire length of International Street, and there were two checkpoints at which pedestrians could cross the international border.

8) The governor of Sonora was Plutarco Elías Calles.

9) The mayor of Nogales, Sonora, was Félix Peñaloza.

Somewhere between 1915 and 1918, either Mayor Félix Peñaloza or Governor Plutarco Elías Calles had the fence erected in an attempt to deescalate growing international tensions.

Those international tensions came to a violent conclusion on August 27, 1918, during the Battle of Ambos Nogales.

Mayor Félix Peñaloza was shot and killed during the battle by US soldiers from the Tenth Cavalry known as the Buffalo Soldiers.

By 1919, the US military had erected a new fence on the US side. Portions of that fence have been torn down and rebuilt over the years, but there are some monument markers from that original fence that still exist today.

The United States made its first major step in establishing a recent border wall between the United States and Mexico in 1993 when then-president Bill Clinton signed into law Operation Safeguard and Hold the Line. These two pieces of legislation were passed by Congress and authorized the construction of fencing along the US-Mexico border in the Arizona and Texas regions.

In 1994, Clinton authorized a third piece of legislation known as Operation Gatekeeper, which allowed construction of fencing along the US-Mexico border in the San Diego, California, region.

Ironically, these three pieces of legislation were enacted to stop the free flow of illegal immigration and drug trafficking.

The Secure Fence Act of 2006, also called HR 6061, was signed into law on October 26, 2006, by then-president George W. Bush. It authorized and funded the construction of seven hundred additional miles of double fencing along the Texas-Mexican border. It means two separate fences with enough room between the two barriers that a border patrol vehicle could drive between the barriers. Then-senators Obama, Clinton, Chuck Schumer (now Senate minority leader), and twenty-three other Democratic senators voted in favor of the act when it passed in the Senate 80–19.

Once again, both the Democrats and Republicans of Congress told the American people that this would help bring an end to the free flow of drugs and illegal immigrants across our southern border. The problem with this is that a continual fence was never completed. If you own a home and a yard, do you put up a fence in the front yard and on one of the sides only? Do you think that a dog would stay in your yard with only two of the four property lines fenced in? No. The dog goes to where there is no fence on your property line and leaves your yard. These illegal aliens are doing the exact thing. They go to where there is no fence and cross into the United States. CONGRESS NEVER FINISHED THE FENCE! I will say this. Bill Clinton and George W. Bush did their part. They had Congress appropriate money, and then they got some of the fence erected. Another problem quickly arose. Shortly after Bush signed Secure Fence Act, the definition of *fence* was redefined. The new definition of *fence* allowed the Department of Homeland Security to determine what type of fence should be used on what type of terrain and topography.

During Obama's first year in office, he erected approximately 130 miles of fencing with money appropriated by Congress from the Bush administration. On May 10, 2011, in El Paso, Texas, President Obama declared that the US-Mexico fence was now "basically complete." He then told the American voters that the US-Mexico border was secure. On that same day of May 10, Sen. Jim DeMint published an article in the *National Review*. DeMint argued that the Obama administration had not finished the fence. In the article, Sen. Jim DeMint stated, "In 2006 legislation was passed to build a 700 mile double layer Boarder Fence along the Texas New Mexico border. This is a promise that has not been kept. Today, according to staff at the Department of Homeland Security, just 5 percent of the double-layer fencing is complete, only 36.3 miles."

Three years later, Barack asked Congress for almost $4 billion ($3.7 billion); but he did not want the money for the continuation and completion of the fence. He was purposely ignoring the completion of the fence/wall. He was still telling the American public that our borders were perfectly safe as is.

On July 8, 2014, the *New York Times* ran this in an article:

President Obama urged Congress on Tuesday to quickly provide almost $4 billion to confront a surge of young migrants from Central America crossing the border into Texas, calling it "an urgent humanitarian situation." The president said he needed the money to set up new detention facilities, conduct more aerial surveillance and hire immigration judges and Border Patrol agents to respond to the flood of 52,000 children. Their sudden mass migration has overwhelmed local resources and touched off protests from residents angry about the impact on the local economy. In a letter to congressional leaders, Mr. Obama urged them to "act expeditiously" on his request."

Senator Marco Rubio of Florida was a very strong opponent to the Obama request of $3.7 billion from Congress. In the article, Rubio gave the following statement, "Let's remember, this administration went around for years saying the border has never been more secure than it is now."

Then senior member of the House Appropriations Committee John Carter of Texas gave this quote to the *New York Times* in that same article, "The president caused this self-inflicted crisis on the border by refusing to enforce the law . . . and now he is requesting a $3.7 billion bailout from the taxpayers to rectify his mistakes."

That's right: *every* president since Bill Clinton has received money from Congress for border wall/fence funding!

Now that Trump wants to make good on his campaign promise, the Democrats will do and say anything to prevent him from completing that task. If you remember back on the campaign trail, Trump predicted all this opposition. When he was talking about draining the swamp of DC politicians, he specifically made it a point of telling you, the voter, that the most powerful people in the most key positions would put up the biggest fight and cause the most problems during his administration. Those people in positions of power do not like having their authority challenged. Their mentality is "How dare he come in here and tell us what we can and cannot do! Doesn't he know that we run the country, not him?"

If you have been paying close attention and hanging on to every word that I have said thus far, you will have noticed that I have not said whether I am a Republican or a Democrat. That's because I am neither. I am an American citizen. I no longer believe in political affiliations. I am an

American citizen. That is all I have to be. I do not have to please anybody other than myself. I make decisions based on what is best for me!

Around twenty-three years ago, my brother, father, and I bought a hunting ranch in the small border town of Brackettville about thirty miles west of Del Rio, Texas. We are approximately thirty miles north of the Rio Grande as the crow flies. That means that I am just a stone's throw away from the Mexican state of Coahuila. I am *directly affected* by illegal migration. In those twenty-plus years, I have always had the occasional illegal immigrants crossing my ranch in groups of two or three. The last time I had an occurrence with the illegal immigrants on my ranch, the group included twenty illegal immigrants and two coyotes. One of the coyotes was carrying a firearm. A coyote" is a paid guide/smuggler. This is the person who leads and navigates the group across the terrain. To put it mildly, the number of illegal immigrants in my part of the country is in the middle of a significant increase.

In the state of Texas, it is illegal to trespass on somebody's property without the landowner's permission. This is a misdemeanor. However, if you are trespassing on a piece of property without the landowner's permission and in possession of a firearm, the charge is upgraded to trespassing in possession of a firearm. That is a felony. Armed people are walking across my property without my consent. While they are walking across my property, they are breaking multiple laws while in possession of firearms such as smuggling humans across an international border. Sometimes they possess bundles of drugs. Sometimes they will sexually assault the females. That, my friends, is aggravated rape. Here in the state of Texas, that is a first-degree felony punishable by five to ninety-nine years in prison.

For the politicians and people who do not have to see this, all this is fine and dandy. It's a little harder for me to turn a blind eye because it's happening on my land.

CHAPTER 7

Drug Epidemic

During the oil-field boom of the eighties, I worked many jobs within the oil-field industry. It is extremely hard physical labor. Many young men enter this field because the oil industry pays top dollar. An average oil-field entry-level position salary pays three to four times the national minimum wage to a high school graduate. In 2019, the United States minimum wage was $7.25. That means the oil-field industry was paying approximately $21.75 for entry-level positions. If you had experience, you can make upward of $40–$50 an hour without a college degree. Plus, depending on what industry you're in, there is abundance of overtime. Make no mistake. This is back-breaking work. This is extremely physically demanding work. There are very few overweight people in the oil-field industry because you must be physically fit. If you do enter the oil-field industry overweight, you will quickly get your body into a physically fit condition. I gladly took the work, and I was paid very well. My body paid the price!

You must remember even though OSHA was founded on April 28, 1971, in the beginning, it only pertained to immediate dangerous work conditions. It's primary focus was to prevent workers from being killed or seriously injured while on the job. Things like back braces, safety glasses, hard hats, hearing protection, and awareness of chemicals did not come to the forefront until the mid-1990s and early 2000s.

In 2007, I saw my first doctor in regard to the condition of my body. I had been living with pain at that time for approximately five years. I was diagnosed with degenerative disc disease. It is a fairly common disease in elderly people—very uncommon for person of my age. What that basically means is I screwed up my spine. Through my years of working in the oil-field-related industries, I added approximately ten to twenty years of age to my spine.

Fast-forward to 2019, I now have seen thirteen doctors including three neurologists. For those of you who do not know what a neurologist is, that is a doctor who specializes in the brain and spine only. I have had countless numbers of X-rays and MRIs. All these doctors are in agreement: my condition is permanent and incurable. That means I will spend every day of the remaining portion of my life in some degree of pain. Some days my pain levels are tolerable, and I can live a normal semblance of life. Other days I need pain medication just to get out of bed. The Texas Department of Public Safety DPS (DMV to all states outside of Texas) has given me handicap license plates for the remainder of my life. I have been fighting the federal government trying to get some type of assistance all to no avail. I have spoken to politicians both state and federal. They seem to be either uninterested or unwilling to assist me. I think it is because they know that I am a member of that very small statistic that throws a monkey wrench in the entire operation of reforming *legal* pain medication laws. I am many times made to feel as if I am a criminal or I am up to nefarious actions when I am having my medications filled.

I find strong similarities between the Carter administration and the Obama administration. The Obama administration had allowed a swell in the illegal immigration from Mexico and Central America. Both of these administrations allowed people from a foreign country to invade the United States and create a drug epidemic. When Carter did it, it was only cocaine. When Obama did it, it was both methamphetamines and opiates. It does not matter that both presidents did this unwittingly or accidentally. The end result was the same: devastation and havoc were wreaked onto the unsuspecting American population.

Do you remember what then senior member of the House Appropriations Committee John Carter said in that New York Times article? "The president caused this self-inflicted crisis on the border by refusing to enforce the law . . . and now he is requesting a $3.7 billion bailout from the taxpayers to rectify his mistakes." When Obama failed to enforce the US-Mexico border laws, he allowed for an influx of illegal immigration, thus, giving free rein to the Mexican drug cartels, allowing them to obtain a stranglehold on the drug and illegal-immigrant smuggling activities into United States. That combined with the fact that the Obama administration is singlehandedly responsible for allowing the major pharmaceutical drug companies the ability to frivolously dispense highly addictive pain medications to people who did not really need them, thus, ensuring that once again America would go through yet another drug epidemic. This current drug epidemic that America is going through belongs solely to the Obama administration and no one else's. This cannot be pinned on the George W. Bush administration or the Trump administration.

Chapter 8

Legal versus Illegal Immigrants

As I mentioned earlier, there are both delusional white and black people who claim that Americans who want to keep illegal immigration in check are racist. Therefore, because I am of the opinion that all illegal immigration needs to come to an abrupt and immediate halt, I am being called a racist. Just to be clear, let me recap. I am a fourth-generation Mexican American citizen who believes that illegal immigrants from Mexico and Central America should not be allowed into the United States unless they come into the United States the proper legal way. Therefore, I'm called a racist. I have even once been called a Nazi. (I never knew that Nazis had Mexican Americans in their organization.)

Keep in mind there is a long line of people who are legally trying to immigrate to the United States. Those people are going through the process in the appropriate manner. Why should they be punished by the activities of illegal aliens who are cutting in line? Why are these illegal immigrants better than legal immigrants? The activities of the illegal immigrants and the current Democratic politicians are a slap in the face and a spit in the eye to all legal immigrants.

I take my hat off and salute all legal immigrants! They go through a life-changing application process. I have seen the civics test that they must complete prior to becoming a citizen. I would venture to say 80 percent of the American population would fail the current civics test administered to all legal immigrants.

When it comes to *legal* immigrants, I believe that they should be required to serve for a minimum of four years in any branch of the armed services prior to receiving citizenship in the United States. Let them prove their loyalty to our nation—their new home. That seems more than a reasonable request, considering all their newly acquired rights and freedoms that they have just obtained. If they are over the age of thirty, they should still be required to join the military in a non-combative military occupational skills (MOS). There are many MOS that do not require massive physical exertion. The military always has a need for cooks, janitors, and motorcade and office personnel.

CHAPTER 9

White and Black Racists

From my perspective, racism is all but dead in America. This is 2019. Everybody is 2,000 percent politically correct. This is the age of political correctness run amok. So I ask you, how can a person be racist when everybody and their brother are looking everywhere for racism?

It does not exist anymore. Maybe that's just because we don't see it here in Texas. I am not saying that there are no racists in Texas. I am more than sure that there is some stupid jackass here in Texas spewing nonsense. What I am saying is that no idiot would be stupid enough to say that out loud here in Texas. We do not tolerate it.

Racism in America is so far gone that the KKK allowed a black journalist W. Kamau Bell the privilege of filming a cross burning. Let me say that again. A black journalist was allowed to film a cross burning at a KKK ceremony. That is something that you don't hear every day.

What that tells me is that membership in the KKK is all but nonexistent. Their membership is so low that they are willing to let a black man into their organization with a camera crew to film their activities in order to bolster their membership. That is a pathetic cry for membership from the KKK.

To all the Caucasian people reading this, you must be aware that there is such a thing as a black racist. This is something that all the black, Mexican, and Asian American people know already. For some reason, there is an extremely large portion of the Caucasian population in America that fails to realize this fact. Of course, a black person will very rarely admit this in front of Caucasians; but from time to time, you will find an honest black person who will tell you the truth regardless of your skin color. Kamau Bell is one of those honest black people. He is so honest that he admits on camera that he has racist people in his family.

NBA Hall of Famer and 1981 NBA Finals MVP Cedric Maxwell was giving an interview about Larry Bird. During that interview, Maxwell admitted that he and most black players at the time in the NBA were racist against white basketball players.

It takes a lot of courage for a black person to say this, reason being if a black person sees another black person telling a Caucasian this, the first black person will immediately call the second black person an Uncle Tom. For those of you who do not know what the term Uncle Tom means, it is an extremely derogatory term hurled from one black person at another. It means that the black person in question has a loyalty to the white man above that of the black race. An Uncle Tom is sometimes referred to as a house nigger.

During his interview, Kamau found out what I have already known for a long time. Racism, while it still exists in small pockets, just typically isn't tolerated in America anymore. Kamau visited multiple subsections of the KKK organization. He found that one of the loudest proponents for the KKK organization is a character named Pastor Thomas Robb. Kamau quickly learned that Pastor Thomas Robb was considered an outcast in his own community of Harrison, Arkansas. Pastor Robb has such an opposition in the town that concerned citizens of the city formed a task force to deal with the shenanigans of Pastor Robb. The town of Harrison is 95 percent Caucasian, and the task force against Pastor Rob is 100 percent Caucasian.

If white people can admit that people like Pastor Robb are idiots, isn't it time that black people equally admit that Al Sharpton and Jesse Jackson are equally idiotic?

The problems we are having in our society today have nothing to do with racism or gender inequality and everything to do with a power struggle. The black activists, gays, and newly empowered feminist women are no longer satisfied with having equality. They each want the upper hand. They want black Americans, feminist women, and gays to have a more than an equal share. That is greed. And that, my friends, is the textbook definition of inequality, racism, and bigotry.

Equal means equal!

A perfect recent example of this is the Jussie Smollett saga. Smollett, who is an openly gay black actor, wanted more money and a bigger role in his TV show. He was blinded by greed and lust for fame and power so badly that he mailed death threats to himself addressed to the TV show. Those letters were turned over to the FBI. He decided that the FBI was not moving fast enough on his case, so he fabricated a hoax about two white people beating him up and putting a noose around his neck in the middle of the night in downtown Chicago during a polar vortex. He claimed that his attackers shouted, "Aren't you that faggot nigger from *Empire*?" and "This is MAGA country." This made national headlines across United States, only to be determined by the Chicago Police Department to be false. It was later discovered that he paid two black men to dress up and attack him. MAGA country in Chicago, Illinois—really? Illinois is the state that Barack Obama served as senator prior to becoming president of the United States.

As if this was not enough, on September 12, 2019, former NFL player Edawn Coughman was arrested by Georgia police. A witness called the police reporting a man breaking into Create & Bake Pizza and Coughman's Creamery. These two businesses are owned by Coughman. The witness reported a vehicle fleeing the scene. The police pulled over a vehicle matching the description only to find out that the vehicle was owned by Edawn Coughman. The police later determined that Coughman was not only wearing gloves but also possessing a crowbar and a can of black spray paint. He was also in possession of the missing items from his establishments. He spray-painted a swastika on a door and then the words *monkey*, *nigger*, and *MAGA* on the walls. It was later discovered that he had called his insurance company to file a claim but failed to call the police.

A sixth-grade twelve-year-old black Virginian girl with dreadlocks claimed that three white boys held her down, covered her mouth, and cut her dreadlocks off while calling her hair ugly and nappy. She claimed that the assault took place on September 23 at Immanuel Christian School in Fairfax County, Virginia. The incident received nationwide coverage. A police investigation was opened only to have the young girl admit that she made the entire story up.

Sirius XM radio show host David Webb was recently accused of having white privilege by CNN legal analyst Areva Martin during the middle of a live radio broadcast. Since Areva is black, her automatic fallback is to play the race card whenever she is losing an argument; so she accused Mr. David Webb of having white privilege. The problem is Mr. Webb is also black. He had the unfortunate pleasure of educating her on this fact live on the air. Areva blamed her staff for not educating her on the fact that Mr. Webb was black prior to the radio interview. I don't understand why a person's skin color should be a factor in prepping for an interview unless the person being prepped is a *racist*!

While I do not believe in the conspiracy theory of white privilege or male privilege, I have been the victim of "Trump derangement syndrome" twice.

The first time I was just verbally berated, and I took it with a grain of salt. The second time it happened, it was a bit more disconcerting because it involved a black female putting her hands on me while she was yelling at me. She was attempting to provoke me into hitting her while we were in the middle of a public library. It was such a surreal experience. I think she was a teenager although she may have been in her early twenties. I have no idea how old she was, although I will say this: she was acting like an insolent twelve-year-old. She was about twelve inches shorter than me, and I outweighed her by about 150 pounds. She kept insisting that I was a racist and a Nazi because I agreed with President Trump on a certain issue.

The problem is that when she put her hands on me without my consent, that is the legal definition of assault or battery, depending on what state you live in. For those of you who are over the age of forty and remember what a dictionary is, the following is a direct passage from a current *Merriam-Webster Dictionary*.

bat·tery

- **1a:** the act of beating someone or something with successive blows: the act of <u>battering</u> (see <u>[1]batter</u>)

> **b** *law*: an offensive touching or use of force
> on a person without the person's consent •
> evidence that supports a charge of *battery* —
> compare [1]assault

If you still do not believe me, please feel free to ask your local police officer.

As I mentioned earlier, I am neither a Republican nor a Democrat. I believe in doing what is best for me as an American citizen. That means sometimes I agree with President Trump, and sometimes I disagree with him. I find it extremely peculiar that whenever I disagree with Trump, the Democrats, SJW, and Far Left people applaud me and cheer me on. However, whenever I agree with him, those same people lose their mind. That's when they show their true colors and immediately throw a temper tantrum and start to accost, browbeat, berate, intimidate, publicly shame, and sometimes assault me.

It's all because I, as an American citizen, sometimes agree with the duly legally elected president of the United States. Since when is it wrong to agree with your sitting president?

These people have no tolerance for ideas that differ from theirs whatsoever. They have no social skills. It literally makes their blood boil that I would have the audacity to have an opinion that is different from theirs. They act like insolent children, thus, the phrase *derangement syndrome.*

In good conscience, I really cannot blame these people for their actions. I blame the Democratic Party and all the leaders within the Democratic Party. For the last three years, the Democratic Party has worked in conjunction with mainstream media and biased tech giants like Google, Facebook, YouTube, and Twitter.

The Democratic Party has manipulated the mainstream media, social media, and the American public. Politicians like Nancy Pelosi, Chuck Schumer, Maxine Waters, Kamala Harris, Cory Booker, Elijah Cummings and Alexandria Ocasio-Cortez have gone in front of cameras and bent, twisted, and contorted the truth. Sometimes they even told boldface lies to the American public. This has gone unchecked for three consecutive years, thus, creating an American public who has been worked into a hysterical frenzy (Trump derangement syndrome or TDS).

I truly feel that these politicians should be held accountable for their actions. It should not be legal for politicians to work the American public into a fever pitch such as this and then be allowed to simply walk away and act as if they had nothing to do with this hysterical community that they created by simply citing freedom of speech as their reasoning for their actions.

I am a *firm believer* in freedom of speech. You must afford all your enemies the right to have their opinions and thoughts heard.

That being said, there are *legal limitations* to freedom of speech, i.e., it is illegal as hell to stand in a crowded movie theater and yell fire at the top of your lungs. You cannot create pandemonium and expect to be exonerated. When you yell fire, everybody starts to immediately run for the exits. All the little people get stampeded by the bigger people because the bigger people are hastily attempting to exit the building. When you falsely yell fire, you endanger the public. These politicians are doing just that—falsely yelling fire!

There are politicians in Washington DC and around the country who do not want to see this country united. Certain politicians want the United States to be divided. They have the same nefarious intentions as the drug cartels—the mentality of divide and conquer. Once the country is divided, these nefarious politicians can manipulate certain subsections of the country.

Case in point: reparations.

—

If the Democratic Party really wanted to pay black Americans reparations, they could have done it during the first two years of Obama's presidency (the 111th Congress, 2009–2011).

During Obama's first two years in office, the White House, the House of Representatives, and the Senate were all controlled by the Democratic Party. In addition to controlling both chambers of Congress and the White House, the Democrats had more than 60 percent of the votes in both chambers of Congress. That was enough to outvote any Republican opposition. That is what is known as a supermajority. They controlled every aspect of the federal government. Nancy Pelosi was the Speaker of the House. The Democratic supermajority came to an end when Republican senator Scott Brown was elected to office.

The Democrats could have overridden any opposition from the Republican Party at that time, and they did on many other issues. The Democratic Party during this time frame shoved law after law after law after law down the American public's throat because they could. The Republicans could do nothing to stop them! Why didn't the Democrats seek reparations during this time frame?

The Democrats did not seek reparations at that time because they don't really want to pay black America reparations. The only reason the Democrats want to talk about reparations now is so that when it gets voted down in Congress, the Democratic Party can holler foul. Then they can say, "Black America, we tried to get you reparations, but the Republicans don't want you to have them."

There have only been three supermajorities in my lifetime, and Democrats had all three of them:

- The Eighty-Ninth Congress (1965–1967)

- The Ninety-Fifth Congress (1977–1979)

- The 111th Congress (2007–2009)

CHAPTER 10

Words of Wisdom

If after reading this you think you live in a racially dominated environment, I have one word for you: *relocate*.

If you were in a bad marriage or relationship, you don't stay there with that person and continue to be miserable. You get a divorce, and you leave. You move on.

I get it—it's sucks.

Nobody said life was fair; and if they did, they were lying to you. Everybody makes bad decisions in their life. If you never made a bad decision, how would you possibly know that you made a good one? You would have nothing to compare it to. In order to appreciate a good laugh, you must truly know how to cry.

Be an adult and accept responsibility for your actions. If you screw up, you say, "I'm sorry." You learn from it, and then you move on. You don't stand there and blame the rest of the world for being who they are just because you failed at something. Maybe you failed because you're incompetent; and it had nothing to do with the color of your skin, sexual orientation, or gender.

My advice to the incompetent person: *become competent*! Stop tearing down society just because you feel that you're not getting your piece of the pie. Start being part of the solution and stop being part of the problem. The world does not revolve around you. Quit worrying about what everybody else has and focus on what you can work to achieve that will make your life more prosperous.

You need to learn how you can contribute to society. In a country such as the United States of America, you only advance on the success of your accomplishments and achievements. Everybody starts at the bottom. Nobody starts at the top. It's called paying your dues.

Find something that you are good at and then figure out how you can make a decent, honest, legal living doing that something. Then find a partner and settle down. Pay your taxes and grow old with your partner.

If you decide to have children, raise, clothe, feed, and _discipline_ them until they have finished their education. Do not dump them on society. Those are your children. You created them, so it is your responsibility to raise them. It is not the responsibility of society to raise your children. Your responsibility as a parent is to be an authoritarian figure, not their friend. If you believe in God, then teach your children about religion.

This country does not owe you anything! Quite the contrary is true. You, as an American citizen, owe this country! All these freedoms and rights that you possess are not free. You pay in the form of being a good citizen and contributing to society. That means taking advantage of the free education that is afforded to you in your youth; getting a job, paying taxes; voting; serving on a jury; enlisting in the military; affording your enemies all the luxuries that you enjoy, i.e., freedom of speech and freedom of religion; participating in the local, state, and federal governments; and assist law enforcement _at all times_. Their job is hard enough. They do not need the added aggravation of dealing with your temper tantrums.

Always remember this: "United we stand, divided we fall."